From Symptoms to Causes

Applying the Logical Thinking Process *to an Everyday Problem*

Thorsteinn Siglaugsson

Contents

Preface

In 2018 I attended a training course in Paris that changed my life. This was H. William (Bill) Dettmer's six-day course in the Logical Thinking Process, an exceptionally powerful methodology for strategy definition and problem solving, based on the methods of Dr. Eli Goldratt, author of The Goal and systems management legend, adapted and refined by Bill Dettmer.

Towards the end of the course I realized how mastering this rigorous methodology changes the way you approach situations of any kind. It helps you deal with difficult situations in a way few if any other methodologies can.

The purpose of this book is to demonstrate, by means of an everyday example, what the Logical Thinking Process is and how powerful it is when it comes to problem solving, as well as provide a short overview of the theoretical foundations it is based on.

This book is not at all meant to be a comprehensive guide for using the process – it is just a primer, but hopefully quite useful as such. Even if it may look simple at first sight, the Logical Thinking Process is a demanding methodology and it takes rigorous training and a good deal of practice to master it. For those interested in learning more about its application I include a short reading list towards the end of the book.

Introduction

The Logical Thinking Process - A game-changer

The Logical Thinking Process is a framework based on the Theory of Constraints Thinking Processes, originally developed by Dr. Eliyahu M. Goldratt, author of bestselling business novel *The Goal* and pioneer of modern production and process management, as a method to improve decision making in the corporate environment. The purpose of Goldratt's framework is to help people make better use of deductive logic to analyze complicated situations and formulate strategy.

Later enhanced, renamed and refined by H. William Dettmer, author of „*The Logical Thinking Process – A Systems Approach to Complex Problem Solving*", the key book on the subject, the Logical Thinking Process is a set of five tools that lead you from defining the goal of your organization or project to mapping the way toward the future. What distinguishes the Logical Thinking Process from most problem-solving and strategy formulation methodologies is its focus on rigorous cause-effect analysis, based on sufficiency and necessity logic, at all stages of the analysis. This is where the alternatives are usually lacking, probably one of the main reasons such a large number of strategy projects eventually fail[1].

But why would someone want to learn how to think logically? We are all able to do so, are we not? In fact, that is mostly true. Most of us can draw correct conclusions from the facts presented to us, identify the fallacy in a simple, wrong, if-then statement, or build a sound deduction from valid assumptions.

However, most of us can do this only to a certain extent, that is, as long as the situation is not too complicated. But in reality, situations very often are.

I recently watched a documentary about Magnus Carlsen, the world champion of chess. Carlsen is a true wonder child. He became grand master of chess when he was thirteen, and at twenty-three, he was world champion. As most of us know chess is a strategic game that relies on logic. The player has to build a strategy and evaluate the possible reactions from the opponent, not only in the next move but many moves ahead. The possibilities soon become so many that most of us give up trying to predict them. This is why chess is so damn hard to become good at.

The most memorable scene from the movie is when Carlsen played against a bunch of highly skilled chess players at Harvard University and won them all.[2] Winning them all was of course an achievement most of us could only dream of. But during the event Carlsen was actually blindfolded. Not only did he have to memorize each position accurately. He also had to formulate in his head his own strategy towards each of his opponents without even having the visual reference of the chess table. What Carlsen was in fact doing was to run in his head several different, highly complicated simulations, systems of if-then statements with probabilities attached to each of those. And due to his experience, one may assume he can often see in an instant where the game is heading without spending time on rigorous analysis. But if an average person tried to predict 10 moves in a chess game nothing much would come out of that.

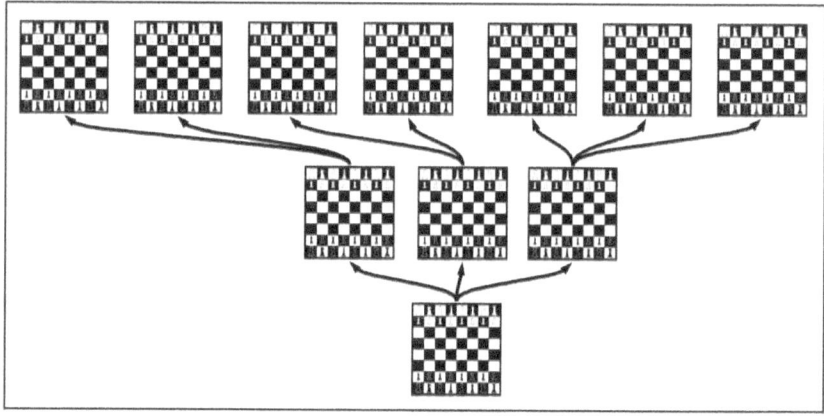

Diagram 1: When playing a game of chess we constantly use logic to evaluate possible outcomes.

But now let's assume they had more time and a simple framework to construct the sequence of possible moves, a tree of cause and effect they could use to visualize the prediction. This would be a game-changer, would it not? With the help of the logical tree structure more or less anyone should be able to predict the 10 moves and in fact the quality of their prediction would probably not be inferior to the quality of Carlsen's prediction.

So, what does this tell us? It tells us is that even if none of us can predict a sequence of moves in our heads like Carlsen does, there is in fact no difference in the ability to understand and formulate the logic as such. It just takes us longer and we need the right tools to do it. For chess is not a mystical game. It is a logical game and therefore, with enough time on their hands, anyone who can think logically can understand the flow of logic in a game of chess.

Now let's think about strategy. Not the strategy of the chessboard, not military strategy, but business strategy. In business, just like in chess, the goal is to win. To outperform the competition. In order to get there, we must build a strategy that takes us to the goal. We must decide our actions and predict the actions and reactions of the competitors. And this we must do many moves ahead just like in a game of chess.

The potential moves are fewer, certainly. But instead we have other complications in business that we don't have in chess. In chess it is just the players and their strategies. In business we also have the market, we have government, we have an external environment we don't control and that can change in unpredictable ways.

And furthermore: On the chessboard we can move the pieces around as we like. The knight will stay where I put it. But the knights, pawns and rooks in our companies are not this easy to deal with. If the human knight puts up passive resistance instead of playing his part in the strategic move, depending on his participation, it may come to nothing. If the pawns rebel, we may have to find a different way forward. In other words, corporate strategy must take into account not only a highly unpredictable external environment, but also the internal environment driven by the apparent chaos of politics, hidden agendas and tacit relationships.

So, if clear logical visualization can enable us to understand the strategy of a chess grandmaster ten moves ahead, what then when it comes to formulating a coherent and logically tight strategy for a company, dealing with an unpredictable external and internal environment? Or analyzing a complex situation to figure out root causes and formulating solutions? In such cases it is a real breakthrough to have a tight framework, based on sound reasoning and rigid testing of hypothesis, to help us build visual, easy-to-understand strategies and analyses.

The Logical Thinking Process is just such a framework. It leads us from the definition of the goal we wish to achieve, provides us with a rigid process to identify the roots of the undesirable effects we experience and expose the faulty assumptions and conflicts that often explain the existence of the root causes. Finally, it provides us with a practical process for formulating a plan towards a solution. All visual and easy to understand. All logically watertight when done correctly.

And no less importantly, the Logical Thinking Process not only helps us structure our own thoughts and analyses. For by visually displaying the links between causes and effects, in a way everyone can understand, it becomes much easier for those not involved in building the analysis to understand it, spot any flaws in the reasoning, and/or add further important refinements. This way the Logical Thinking Process is actually a very strong framework to enhance collaboration and improve communication.

The Logical Thinking Process is a framework that helps us to take better advantage of our ability to think logically, a tool that helps us cut through the complexity of a situation – just like a visualized sequence of chess moves would enable us to understand the player's strategy – and to communicate our insights to others in a clear and compelling way.

The Logical Thinking Process
An overview

Every human organization is a system. And as they grow, they become more complicated. What characterizes such a system is that an event that takes place in one area affects other areas of the system, and the way this happens is very often not evident. In other words, there is always a chain of causality, and this chain is not always easy to follow. This means that decisions we make can often have effects that are not easily predictable. Sometimes, formal organizational structure and chains of command cloud the true causality and create incentives that direct us away from trying to understand it.

Secondly, it is common - far too common - that our decisions are based on wrong assumptions. Wrong assumptions are harmful, for they reflect an incorrect view of reality. Sometimes those assumptions are tacit - we do not realize we make them. Sometimes we are fully aware of them, but we do not understand the negative impact they have on our decisions, and hence on our system. Finally, we can be aware of the paradigms and also aware of their harmful consequences, but unable to find an alternative. Deciphering the causality, unearthing false assumptions and removing the conflicts behind false paradigms; this is what the Logical Thinking Process helps us to do.

In other words, the Logical Thinking Process is designed to help us make better decisions. The process is comprised of five steps, based either on necessity or sufficiency reasoning. The logical rigor is really the key to this whole process and what sets it apart from most other such methodologies. In addition to the five steps, an integral part of the methodology is a comprehensive checklist, used to verify the validity of each entity and cause-effect connection in the analyses.

The first step, the *Goal Tree*, is used to define a single goal we aim to achieve and what is necessary to get there. The next step is the *Current Reality Tree*, which we use to analyze why we have not already reached the goal. The third step is to solve conflicts that prevent us from attacking root causes of problems. Once this is done, we move on to define the path towards the future using a *Future Reality Tree* and a *Prerequisite Tree*. The Future Reality Tree is used to map out what has to be achieved and precisely how they are sufficient to reach the goal. The Prerequisite Tree is used to define the individual steps.

It depends on the task at hand whether one goes through the whole process or picks out individual parts. Sometimes it is enough to build a Goal Tree. This might be the case when dealing with a new project for example or when setting up a new business. In other cases, one might jump right into a Conflict Resolution Diagram, and in yet others, if the goal is already very well defined, the Current Reality Tree might be the starting point.

Since the purpose here is to explain the process as a whole, I will go through all the steps to demonstrate how the five tools work and how they are linked together.

In my opinion the best way to make an abstract theory clear and understandable is to use everyday examples. So, this is what I do here. The example I use is not a complex business case, but a very generic situation from daily life that everyone can understand and relate to. We might keep in mind, that the Logical Thinking Process is not only meant for solving complex business problems, it is in fact a framework that can be used for any kind of situation, though its value increases with the complexity of the situation we encounter.

I split the discussion into a series of short chapters. First I discuss how to structure a Goal Tree. Then how to analyze a problem to get to a root cause, using a Current Reality Tree. The third part explains the use of a Conflict Resolution Diagram to break up conflicts that often explain why we have the root cause in the first place. In the fourth chapter I discuss how we structure solutions using a Future Reality Tree and a Prerequisite Tree. In the fifth and final chapter I wrap up the discussion and explain the theoretical foundations of the Logical Thinking Process.

In Appendix A at the end of the book you will find a few further examples of the application of the Logical Thinking Process tools. Appendix B contains a comprehensive overview of the process.

What is our goal?

Using the Goal Tree to define the goal we strive for and what is necessary to reach it

The problem

The problem I want to solve has to do with my house. The house looks shabby, there is bad smell from the drain in my laundry, my lawn looks bad and the pavement is uneven. My goal is to have a neat looking and well maintained house, and a beautiful garden that is also well sheltered, in short, a house my neighbors admire. But there is a gap between what I want and what I have.

Let's start by structuring the issue a bit, at least I want to visualize how the problems I described lead to the fact that my house and garden are shabby. We see this in *Diagram 2*: the reasons below and the result at the top.

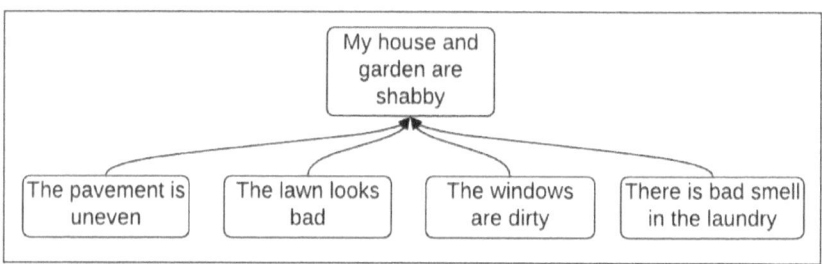

Diagram 2: What makes my home shabby?

Now, the first thing most of us would immediately do is go directly to the possible solutions. Water the lawn, clean the windows and so on, as we see in *Diagram 3*. We do this by instinct – there is a problem – we try to solve it. But the issue with this common approach is that we keep fixing the effects, not the causes, and often we don't really know if the solutions will work, even in the short term, and may have no idea if they might have unintended negative side-effects. Is the reason for the appearance of the lawn really the lack of water and fertilizer, or are there other possible causes? Cleaning the windows will certainly make them clean, but how fast do they become dirty again? Is there some specific reason this happens?

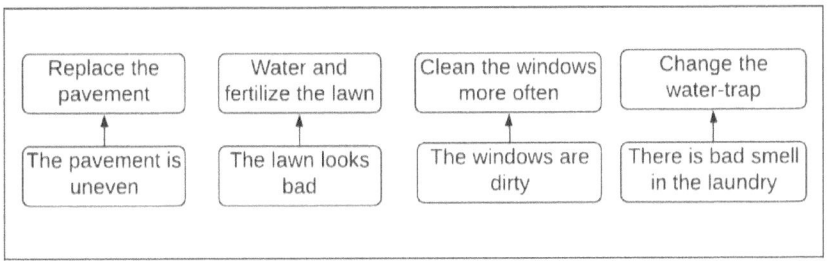

Diagram 3: Jumping to conclusions.

In other words, we tend to skip the analysis and take shortcuts, very often without really knowing if they will work, let alone that they will address the real causes. And it is here that we find the first difference between the Logical Thinking Process and the common approach.

Step 1: The Goal Tree

In fact, there is no platform for shortcuts of this kind within the framework of the Logical Thinking Process. We don't even start by analyzing the problems. Instead, the first thing we do is to define where we want to be. To do this we construct a *Goal Tree*. The Goal Tree is used to define the ultimate goal we want to achieve, define what *critical success factors* must be in place to reach the goal, and which *necessary conditions* must be fulfilled to achieve them.

The success factors are critical because if any one of them is not fulfilled we will not reach our goal. We call this a *necessary relationship*.

The Goal Tree is key to the whole analysis. The reason is that when we want to solve problems we must first have a clear picture of where we are heading and what is required to get there. Otherwise we will lack the focus necessary to make sure we actually solve the right problems.

We see the Goal Tree for our example in *Diagram 4*. At the top we have the goal; A house my neighbors admire. Right below we have the critical success factors necessary to reach the goal. Below those are the necessary conditions for achieving the critical success factors. We read the Goal Tree from the top and down. Each arrow indicates the necessary relationship between the entities it connects. Example: "In order to have a beautiful garden I must have a well maintained lawn and a neat garden".

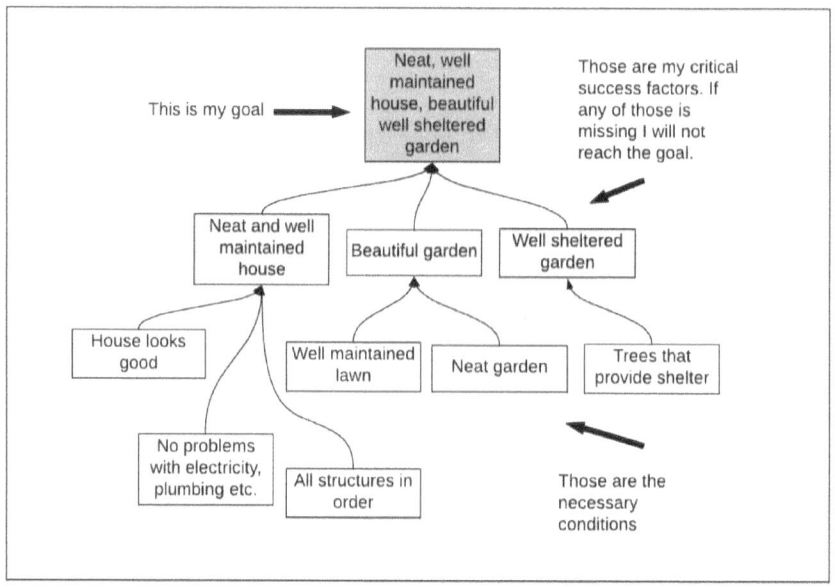

Diagram 4: The Goal Tree.

Now I have stated the goal and defined what is necessary in order to reach it. In the next chapter I discuss how we use the next step in the Logical Thinking Process to find out why I am not reaching the goal.

At first sight, constructing a Goal Tree looks like a really simple exercise. But in reality, it is a lot more demanding. The first challenge is to define the goal. In an organization it is not uncommon that people have many different versions of what the goal of the organization should be. And even if they broadly agree it is very common that the stated goal is unclear, even consisting of several conflicting sub-goals.

Secondly almost everyone will at first have trouble with following the necessity logic of the Goal Tree. We are very used to listing out requirements for a goal without really considering the difference between a necessity and a nice-to-have. But the logical structure of the Goal Tree requires us to get rid of everything that is not crucial. This is also why the Goal Tree is so important as a first step in improvement projects - it directs the focus towards the problems that are important and away from those that really don't have to be solved at all.[3]

Finding the root cause

Using sufficiency logic to find the root of the problem

In the preceding chapter I demonstrated how to build a *Goal Tree* to determine all the conditions necessary to achieve the goal of having a house my neighbors admire. Now that we have defined our goal, the *critical success factors* for reaching the goal, and the *conditions necessary* to fulfill them, we know what I need to have. We also know I don't have those things now.

Step 2: The Current Reality Tree (Problem Tree)

In the second step of the Logical Thinking Process we analyze the problems to find what causes them. For this we use the *Current Reality Tree.*

We start by listing the problems. Those will usually be based on critical success factors and necessary conditions from the Goal Tree: I want a beautiful garden, but the grass does not grow properly, and the lawn is scattered with leaves. I want a well maintained and neat house, but my house is shabby, and it looks as if something might be wrong with the plumbing.

We use the term *undesirable effects* for the issues. Why? Because very often, what we call problems, are not really the true problems. They are rather consequences of some underlying causes, which are the real problems: A bad smell in the laundry is not the problem in itself, for if it were, I would just cover the drain, and the problem would go away. But of course it won't. The smell is only an <u>undesirable effect</u> - a symptom of an underlying problem.

In *Diagram 5,* we see the undesirable effects at the top, and below them we start listing the possible causes. Notice the ellipse around two of the arrows. It indicates that put together, the two causes right below the effect, are sufficient to produce it.

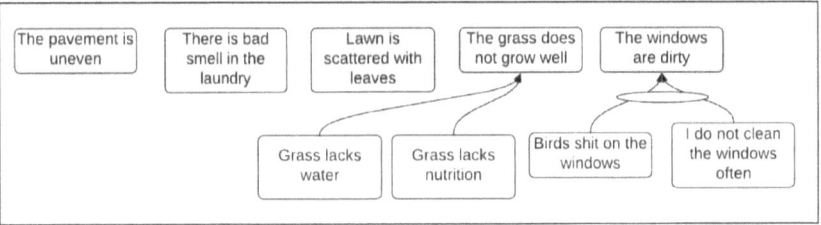

Diagram 5: Current Reality Tree. First step: Trying out some possible causes.

Note especially the point regarding water and nutrition, for this is really what we originally listed as a potential solution in *Diagram 3* in the previous chapter, But as we move on with the analysis, we will see why lack of water and nutrition is not in fact the cause of the bad shape of the lawn, for when using the Logical Thinking Process we always check each entity and each logical connection for validity. And in this case, it so happens that we actually know there really is no lack of water and nutrition. Therefore, this cannot possibly be the cause.

Digging out the roots

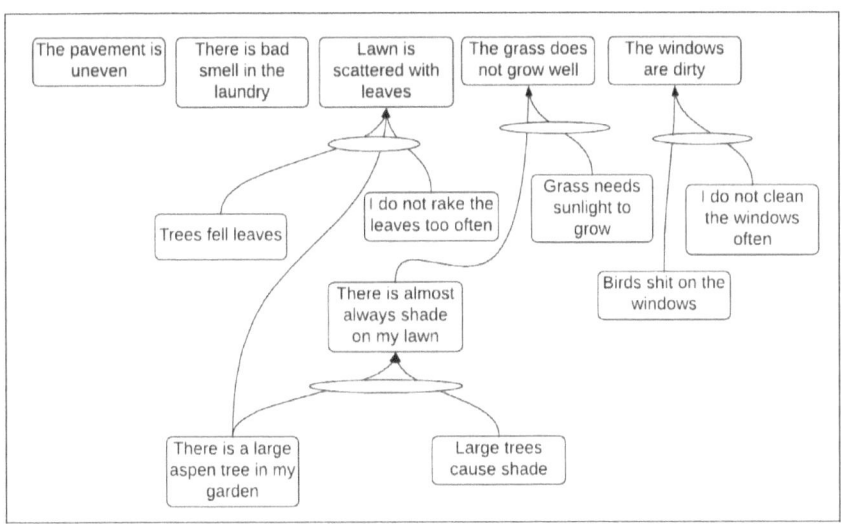

Diagram 6: Deepening the analysis.

In *Diagram 6* we keep deepening our analysis, filling in what we find out as we investigate the issues. We have removed the incorrectly suggested cause of the problem with the lawn and found a more plausible one. We deepen our analysis, but obviously we still have some way to go. We know now why the lawn is scattered with leaves. We also see the same cause is behind the shade on the lawn. It is the tree in our garden, as we see in *Diagram 6*. Notice the form of the reasoning: There is shade on the lawn AND grass needs sunlight to grow, THEREFORE it does not grow well. Both premises are needed for the conclusion to be valid and they are sufficient to produce the effect. This type of reasoning is called a syllogism, and sufficiency-based logic trees like the Current Reality Tree are rife with them.

But we don't yet know why the birds leave droppings on the windowsills. And we still need further analysis to figure out the reason for the smell in the laundry and the uneven pavement.

We start by removing a bit of pavement to check what might cause it to be uneven. Beneath we find tree roots. So, clearly, the tree is spreading its roots quite widely. And how about the windows? Isn't it likely that the tree attracts the birds that shit on the windows? And since the roots push up the pavement, is it possible they also have ruined the sewer pipes, causing the smell? Let's finish our Current Reality Tree with *Diagram 7*: The finished Current Reality Tree shows us how the undesirable effects can be traced back to a single root cause; a large aspen tree in my garden.

What we see here is a manifestation of something very common: Seemingly unrelated problems in fact have a common cause. Of course, there is not always a single cause behind all our problems. But often, a surprising proportion of the undesirable effects will have the same root cause. And it is only by removing the root causes that we can get rid of the undesirable effects they produce. In other words: As long as a cause remains, we will not eliminate the undesirable effects it causes.

We have now found a single root cause. In the next chapter we will see why we have this root cause and what we can do about it.

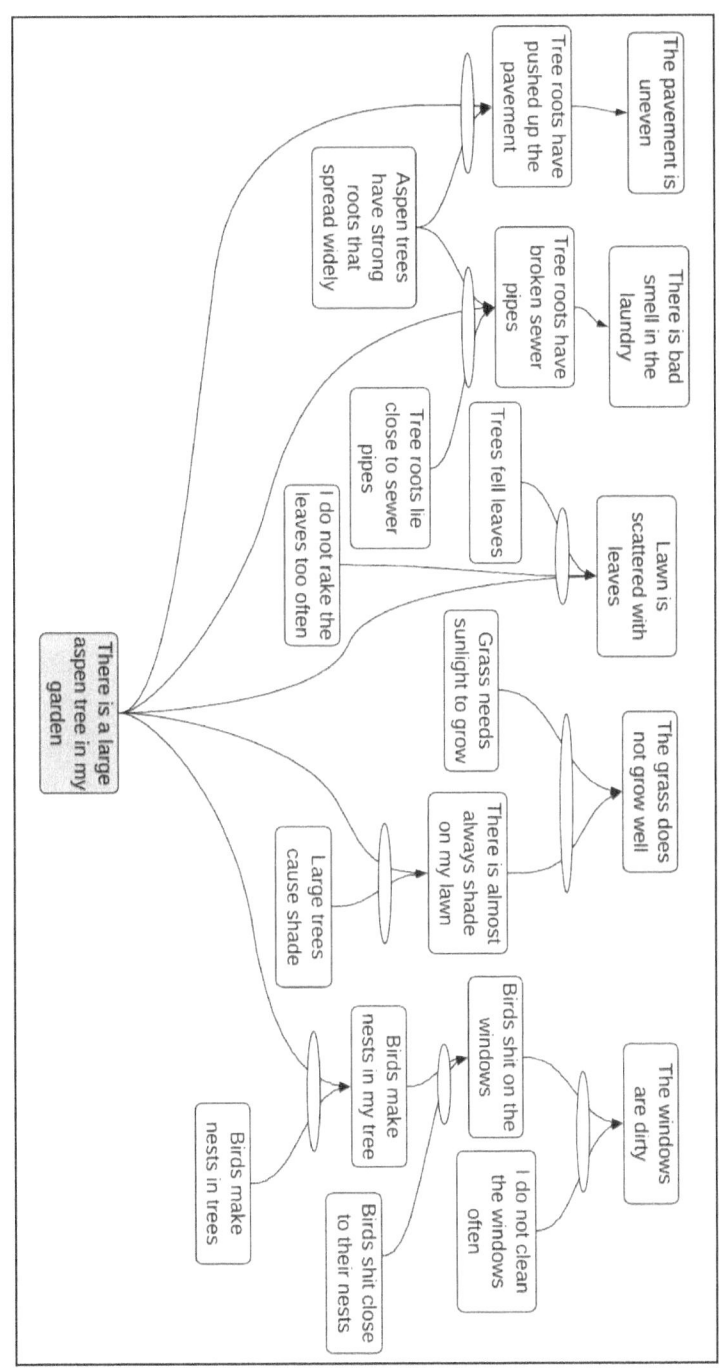

Diagram 7: The full Current Reality Tree.

Solving the conflict

How to use a Conflict Resolution Diagram to structure and solve an underlying conflict

Now we have identified an aspen tree in the garden as the root cause of all the issues that prevent me from reaching my goal of having a house my neighbors admire. So, what am I waiting for? Let's chop it down! Case closed!

Or is it perhaps not as simple as this?

Remember, one of the critical success factors is to have a well sheltered garden. In fact, this is the tree that provides the shelter. In addition, it is really beautiful. So, I'm not all that eager to cut it down after all.

In other words, I have a conflict. I suspect I have to do A, but at the same time I'm reluctant to do it, because I also feel I need B, which is the opposite of A. If you think about it for a moment you will certainly recognize many such situations both from work and personal life. And when conflicts don't go away the reason is that we don't really know how to solve them - they just sit there, and we learn to live with them. Which is perhaps not such a good thing.

We know the aspen tree causes all those problems, but it is beautiful, and it provides shelter. Still, I need to get rid of all the undesirable effects, so I cannot let the conflict stop me from doing that. The only way, therefore, is to dissolve the conflict. And this can only be done if, using rigorous reasoning, we can find some inherent flaws in it. For this we use the *Conflict Resolution Diagram,* which constitutes the third step in the Logical Thinking Process. We see it in *Diagram 8.*

Step 3: The Conflict Resolution Diagram

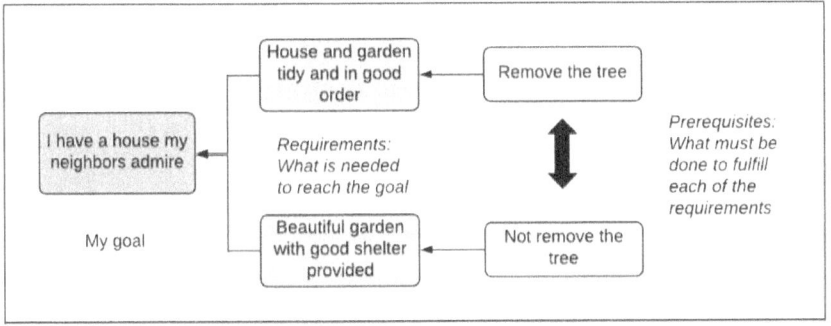

Diagram 8: Structuring the conflict.

The Conflict Resolution Diagram is composed of five entities: On the left we see the ultimate goal we wish to reach. Then we have the requirements that need to be fulfilled in order to reach the goal. In our case one requirement is a tidy house and garden in good order, and the other is a beautiful garden with good shelter provided. On the right we have the prerequisites for each requirement.

As we see, in order to reach the goal, we have to fulfill two requirements, and both are necessary – without both we will not reach the goal. But we cannot fulfil both or at least it seems so. To have a house my neighbors admire, I must remove the tree, but at the same time the tree provides the shelter and adds to the beauty of the garden, so therefore I must keep it.

This conflict is what has kept me from doing anything about the problem. But now we have structured the conflict. That means we can start trying to solve it. The first step is to list the assumptions behind the logical connections. Why are the two requirements necessary to reach the goal? Why are the two prerequisites needed to fulfil the requirements? We see all those assumptions in *Diagram 9*.

We have the assumptions, and now deductive logic comes to our assistance again, for the third step in this analysis is to use rigorous reasoning to scrutinize the assumptions in order to figure out if any of them might be invalid. First, we look at the connections between the goal and the two requirements. We see right away that the cause-effect relationship is valid. Then we focus our attention on the assumptions behind the connections between the requirements and the prerequisites.

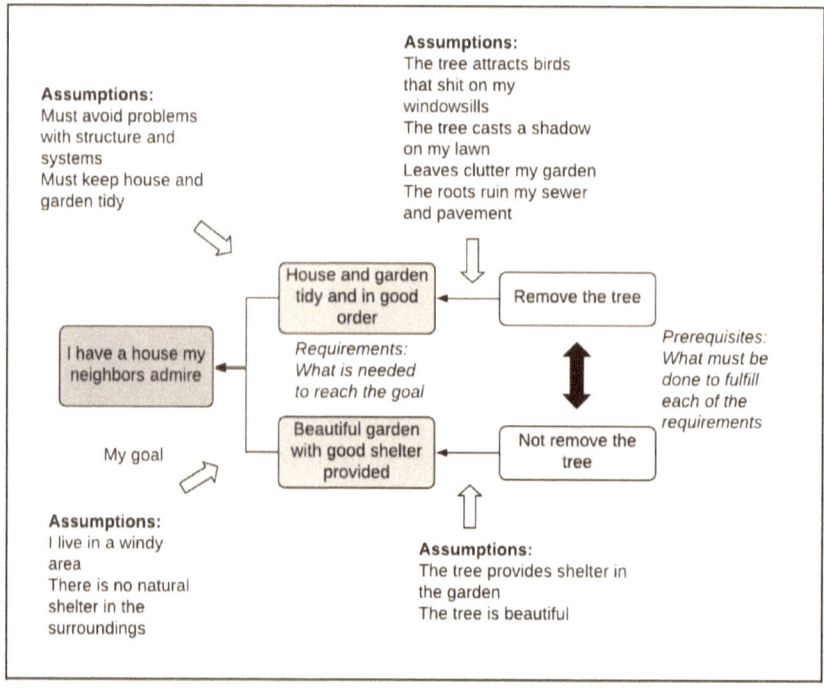

Diagram 9: The assumptions behind the conflict.

The reasons for removing the tree are all causal relationships we identified in our Current Reality Tree, described in the previous chapter. Those are all valid; as long as I have the tree, I will necessarily have those problems. Not removing the tree has two underlying true assumptions: The tree is beautiful, and it provides shelter. But are they valid?

Are the assumptions valid?

Now we must remember it is not enough for the assumptions to be factually true. They must also necessarily lead to the prerequisite. In other words we must be able to say: „Without this particular tree I will necessarily lose those two desirable outcomes."

Therefore, it is not enough to state that the tree is beautiful and provides shelter, for this does not really mean we absolutely have to have this tree ... Instead we must define the <u>exact</u> assumptions that lead to the unavoidable need to keep precisely this tree.

In other words, for the cause-effect relationship to be valid, it must be valid that <u>only this tree</u> can provide the shelter needed, and that <u>no other tree</u> can possibly be beautiful. So, we must add those two assumptions to fulfil the requirement for a necessary relationship.

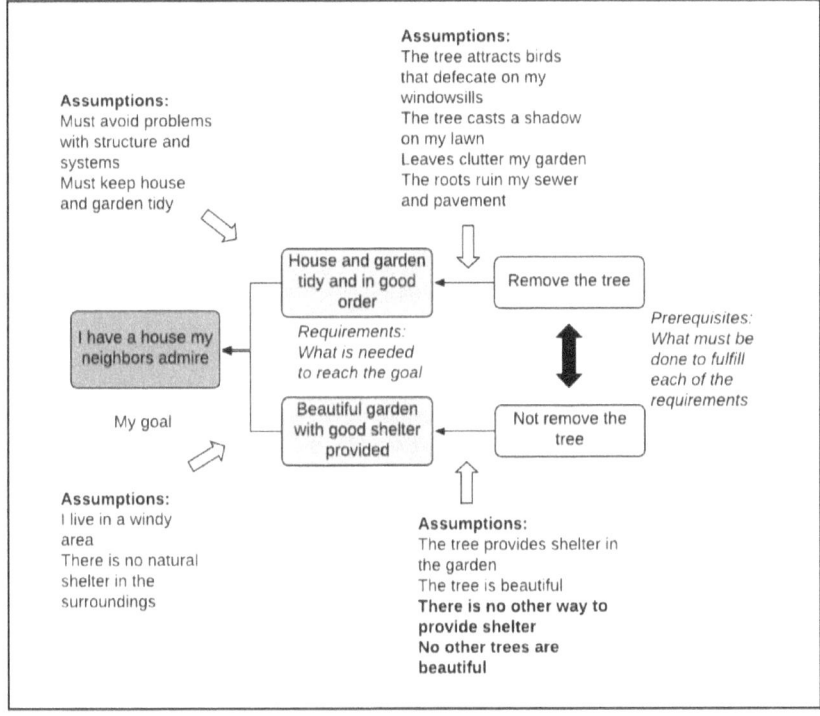

Diagram 10: Surfacing hidden assumptions.

What we are doing here is surface hidden assumptions that were <u>clouded</u> for lack of clarity. And we don't have to look at them twice to see they are false. We see them in bold in *Diagram 10*.

Sometimes this is the case: The assumptions we have made are not really strong enough to necessarily lead to the prerequisite, so we must rephrase or surface new ones to get the clarity needed. In other cases, we may have assumptions that are clear, but simply wrong.

This is how the Conflict Resolution Diagram helps us surface invalid assumptions, by means of rigorous necessity reasoning. No compromises, no vague connections, no unclear entities are allowed. And if we try to cut corners, others, to whom we demonstrate our findings, will pinpoint the flaws soon enough.

The Injection

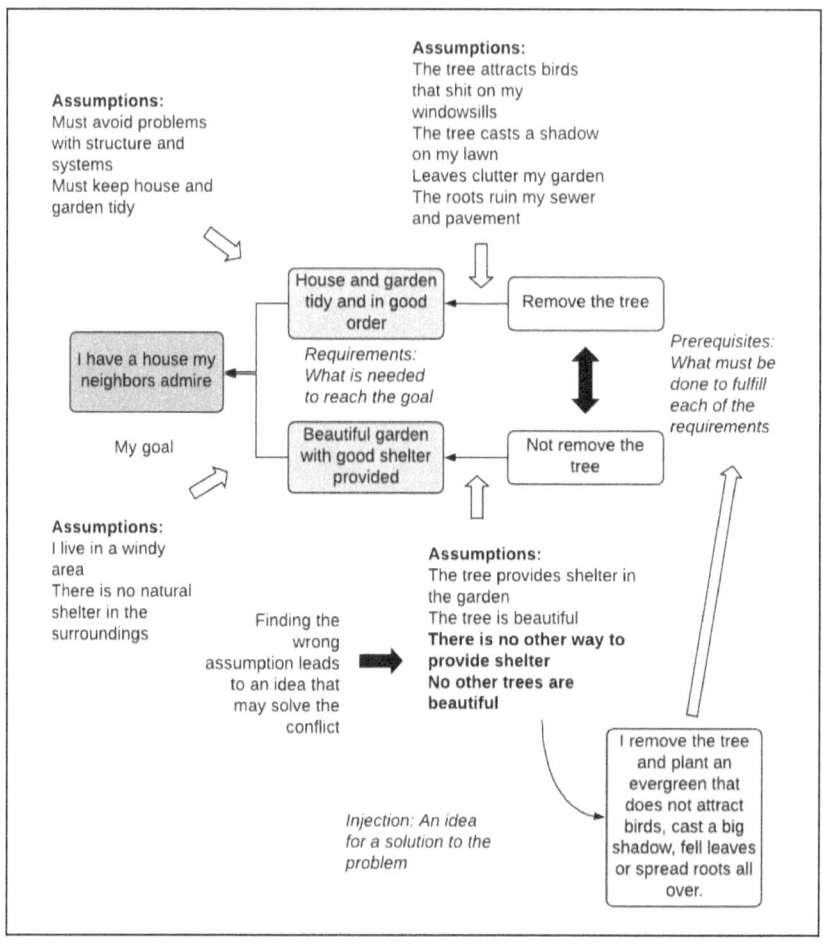

Diagram 11: The Injection.

So, after adding the clarified assumptions, we have identified that one of the prerequisites is in fact not supported. The reason being that the valid assumptions that remain are not sufficient to support it: We don't need precisely this tree after all. Yet, we definitely need something, for the requirements are still there, and those must still be fulfilled. Therefore, the next step is to find a solution that fulfils both requirements and at the same time invalidates the conflict. We call this solution an *injection*.

An injection is an idea for a solution that solves the conflict. Our injection is to remove the aspen tree and plant a new, less problematic tree that is also beautiful and that provides shelter. We need this new tree to be free from scattering leaves everywhere and spreading roots all over, and it must be a species that does not attract birds. We decide to plant an evergreen. We see the injection on the right side in *Diagram 11*.

Sometimes we are quick to come up with an injection. In other cases, it requires hard work. But by going through the rigorous analysis required by the Conflict Resolution Diagram, we have stripped away all vague and wrong assumptions. This is of immense importance, for then we know precisely which requirements the solution must fulfill, and which not – there is no guesswork allowed.

What we are really doing here is to distinguish between needs and wants. We <u>want</u> to have the tree, but it is the requirements that state our real <u>needs</u>. And it is the needs that matter.[4]

Having solved the conflict means we are well on our way towards our goal. But we are not there yet. Now we must find out if the injection really leads to a workable solution. Perhaps we have to find a different one. Perhaps we need to add something more to achieve our goal. The final step in the process is to use a *Future Reality Tree* and *Prerequisite Tree* to finish our work.

But before we move on, why not think for a moment about some long-standing problem you may have encountered at work? Something that comes up again and again, that is regularly discussed in meetings. Something everyone agrees has to be fixed, but that somehow just seems to hang in there. Think about why this is the case. Is it possible you may have a conflict, a disagreement, explicit or hidden, not about where you want to go, but about what you need to get there? Might there be a faulty policy in place? Might it even be a personal issue? Then try to plug it into a *Conflict Resolution Diagram* and surface the assumptions. The results might be revealing.

Toward the future

Using a Future Reality Tree and a Prerequisite Tree to map the way forward

The goal is to have a house my neighbors will admire. And we have built a *Goal Tree* to define the *Critical Success Factors* and *Necessary Conditions* for achieving the goal.

In the second step we used a *Current Reality Tree* to analyze why we were not reaching our goal, and identified a large aspen tree in the garden as the source of all our troubles.

In the third step we found a way to fulfill both the need to provide shelter and beauty in the garden, and the need to avoid all the problems caused by the aspen tree, that has ruined the sewer and pavement, clutters my garden with leaves, casts shade on the lawn and attracts birds that shit on my windows. To do this we used a *Conflict Resolution Diagram* to take our focus away from the <u>wants,</u> and towards the real <u>needs</u>. Now it looks as if I have a solution to my problem. I remove the aspen tree and plant an evergreen.

Step 4: The Future Reality Tree (Solution Tree)

But we are not done yet. Now we need to verify that this solution will actually solve my problems. For this we use a tool called a *Future Reality Tree*. We also need to verify that the solution does not generate some new problems, and if it does, we must amend it, find a different one, or take some additional actions to overcome the new problems. Finally, we have to figure out if anything more is needed to reach the goal. Is the injection from our Conflict Resolution Diagram enough, or do we need some additional injections?

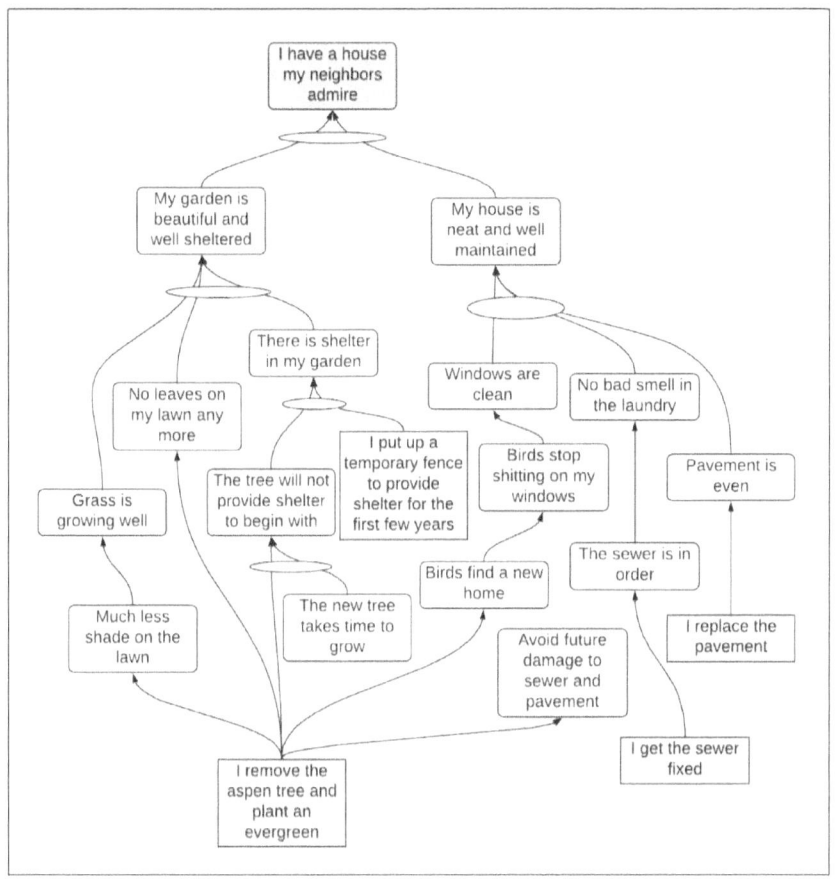

Diagram 12: The Future Reality Tree.

Now it is clear that the aspen tree causes all the problems identified. By removing it the lawn will recover, the leaves will stop cluttering my backyard and the birds will stop leaving their droppings on the windowsills. But removing the tree will however not by itself repair the damage to the sewage and the pavement. It will prevent further damage, but what has already occurred must still be fixed. This is why we need two more injections related to this; we must have the sewer pipes replaced and we must fix the pavement. All this we see in *Diagram 12*.

When constructing a Future Reality Tree, it is important to look for any negative effects that might be caused by the solution. Those can be unintended side-effects which, in the terminology of the Logical Thinking Process, are called *Negative Branches*. If we have a Negative

Branch that is serious enough, we must find new injections to solve, or "trim" it. Sometimes the solution can actually cause a vicious cycle, called a *Negative Reinforcing Loop*. When that happens, we must discard the solution and find a new injection.

The negative branch here is that once the tree is gone there will be some time until the new one provides the shelter needed. To trim this negative branch, we decide to put up a temporary fence for shelter until the evergreen is tall enough. Looking at the Future Reality Tree now, we see how the injections lead directly to the solution. All the injections together are sufficient to solve the problems and reach the goal.

Step 5: The Prerequisite Tree (Implementation Tree)

While the Future Reality Tree shows how we will reach the goal, sometimes we encounter obstacles when it comes to implementing the solutions. Some of the injections may require a detailed implementation plan to unveil and tackle those obstacles. In our example we may assume this is true for all the injections. We may not have all we need to remove the tree, fixing the sewer and replacing the pavement will require careful project planning.

This is where the final step in the Logical Thinking Process, the *Prerequisite Tree*, comes in handy. The purpose of the Prerequisite Tree is to construct a step-by-step implementation plan for a part of the Future Reality Tree and unveil and handle the obstacles that are in the way.

Diagram 13 shows a simple Prerequisite Tree for the key injection we used to solve our conflict – removing the tree and planting a new one. Removing a large tree is a complex task and must be performed safely and using the proper tools.

In our case we don't have the chainsaw required, we don't have a truck to take away the tree and we don't have a new tree to plant. Once we construct the plan, step-by-step, we unearth those obstacles and find the ways to address them.

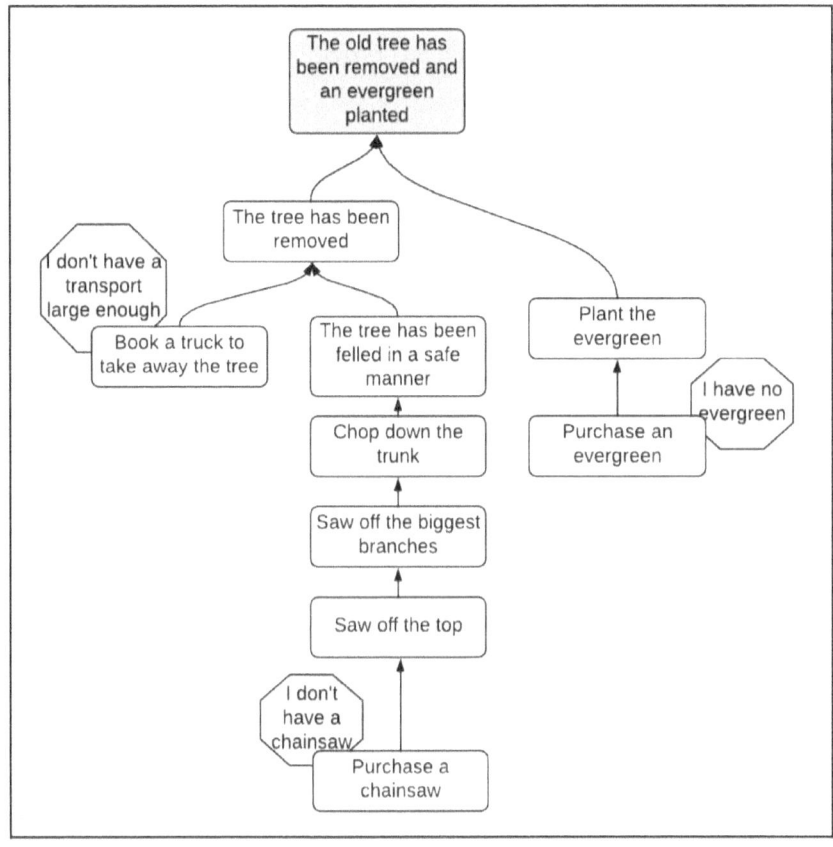

Diagram 13: The Prerequisite Tree.

We have now used the Logical Thinking Process to find a lasting solution to the problems I encountered with my house and garden. We finish off the work by creating the Prerequisite Tree and in fact if we lay it on its side, we already have the skeleton for a project plan!

	Day1		Day2	Day3	
Preparation	Purchase a chainsaw				
Cutting down the tree		Saw off the top	Saw off the biggest branches	Fell the tree	Chop down the trunk	
Removing the tree	Book a truck				Remove tree
Planting				Plant evergreen	

Diagram 14: A simple project plan.

We have seen how one step in the process leads directly to the next and hopefully this simple example has provided some insight into how powerful this process is.

But what makes it this powerful? And why does it give those who master it such an advantage when it comes to complex problem solving?

Pulling it all together

What is it that makes the Logical Thinking Process such a powerful methodology?

The purpose of the simple example described in the preceding chapters is to demonstrate how The *Logical Thinking Process* tools form a powerful framework for establishing goals, identifying root causes, dissolving conflicts and designing lasting solutions. When dealing with complex situations, this structured approach becomes even more valuable.

A unified process

We have seen how a simple everyday problem can be solved effectively using the Logical Thinking Process. What about when it comes to finding out why our company is losing money, why wait times in our hospital keep increasing, or why our factory keeps piling up inventory? In such cases we need a rigorous process to help untangle the situation, and this is precisely what the Logical Thinking Process is.

Diagram 15 shows a simplified example of a typical business problem. Here, the goal is a bigger and more profitable business. The root cause that prevents us from reaching the goal is a narrow, limited product line. Behind that lies the conflict between investing in more capacity and saving money. The injection is to make better use of existing capacity to expand the product line and enter new markets.

We use the *Goal Tree* to define where we want to go and what we have to do to get there. The Goal Tree is really a key to the whole process for two reasons: First, because we have to know where we are heading to be able to move on towards the future. Second because the Goal Tree requires us to figure out what is necessary to achieve the goal, and only what is necessary. This way the Goal Tree helps us <u>focus</u> on the real critical success factors and leave out all the nice-to-haves.

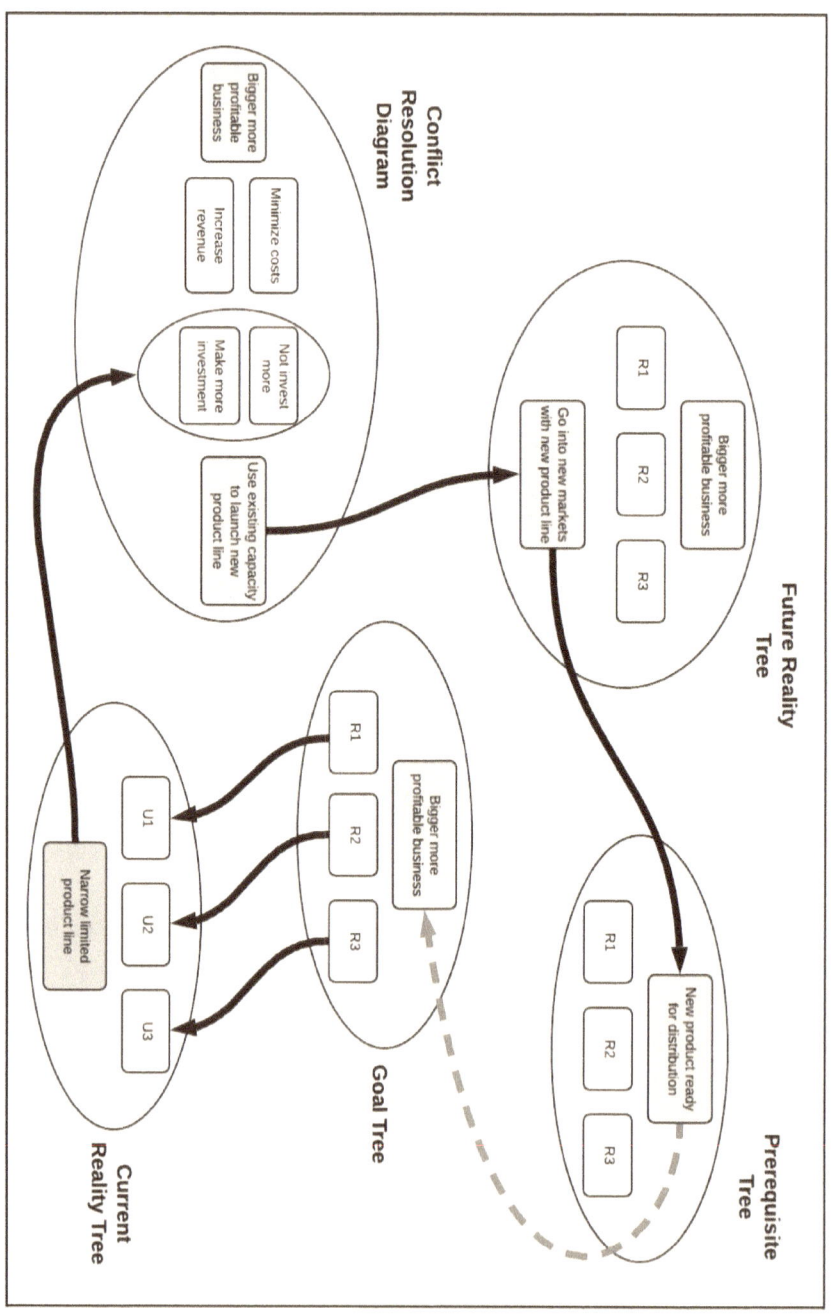

Diagram 15: Overview of a business problem solution

Once we have identified the critical success factors and seen where we need to improve, we start the problem solving, using the *Current Reality Tree*. Here the focus is on find all the things that contribute to the problems, either individually or together. We do not stop until we have reached the root causes.

Here again valid sufficiency relationship is the key. We look for a cause or combination of causes sufficient to directly produce the effect.

Very often a root cause identified in the Current Reality Tree will be based on a conflict between different ways to reach the same objective. Sometimes those are based on policies, sometimes on different approaches, sometimes personal agendas play a part. The Conflict Resolution Diagram helps us to unearth the invalid assumptions that produce the conflict.

Once the invalid assumptions have been found we find an injection, a new idea that can become the solution we need to reach the goal. Then we use the *Future Reality Tree* to determine precisely how the injection enables us to reach the goal. The Future Reality Tree is based on sufficiency logic; we must make sure each step towards the solution is based on sufficient premises.

Finally, we use the *Prerequisite Tree* to map out precisely the road towards the solution and unearth any obstacles that are in the way.

It may be interesting to think of the example presented here as an analogy with typical organizational problems. Let's say the plumbing stands for our production facility that is not operating optimally. Let's think of the lawn as our sales department and the bird droppings as customer complaints we constantly try to "wipe away" but that always reappear. Then let our reluctance to remove the tree stand for outdated management practices that drive sub-optimal behavior, affecting every area in the organization. Finally, we might see our requirement for shelter as the deep-rooted need for security that causes our resistance to change, even when we know the error of our ways.

The Logical Thinking Process has been used by businesses for over 25 years to analyze and find solutions to such problems. If you learn how to use the framework and practice at it, it is amazing how quickly it becomes an integral part of how you approach complex problems and present your ideas and analyses. And you will be surprised when you experience the advantage it gives you.

So, what makes it this powerful?

In my opinion the key strengths of the Logical Thinking Process are the following:

1. The requirement for clarity and sound reasoning at all stages of the analysis vastly improves the quality of our analyses and strategy formulation efforts.

2. Detailed visual presentation, which means any flaws can be unveiled almost instantly once the analysis is presented to a wider audience.

3. Tight links between the five tools –the analysis at each stage directly links into the next one, which provides a coherent, seamless framework.

4. The tools allow us to present highly complicated problems and solutions in an easy-to-understand manner.

5. The requirement for precision helps improve communication by lowering the probability of misunderstanding, a key source for arguments and harmful differences.

Aristotelian logic

The Logical Thinking Process is based on five key principles: First, Aristotle's principle of valid deduction, or syllogism, that is, the requirement that the assumptions behind a conclusion are sufficient. A classical syllogism contains two premises, a minor and major premise, and a conclusion necessarily based on those premises. A well known example I still remember from my days as a philosophy undergraduate is:

Premise 1: All men are mortal.

Premise 2: Socrates is a man.

Conclusion: Socrates is mortal.

When we look at the logic trees used by the Logical Thinking Process we will find syllogisms all over the place. Let's look at the Current Reality Tree for example. The reason my windows are dirty is that the birds shit on the windows. But this alone does not mean they will always be dirty. I might clean them every day for example. So, for a valid syllogism we need both premises:

Premise 1: Birds leave droppings on my windowsills.

Premise 2: I do not clean my windows too often.

Conclusion: My windows are dirty most of the time.

Secondly, the framework requires necessity logic when this is applicable. The example above shows us sufficiency logic; it is sufficient to keep my windows dirty that I don't clean them, and the birds shit on them. But they are not necessary, for something else than bird droppings might make my windows dirty[5]. If we look at the assumptions in the Conflict Resolution Diagram, we will find more examples of necessity logic: For the prerequisite of not removing the tree to hold, for example, it <u>must</u> be true that only this tree provides shelter and only this tree is beautiful. Those are necessary conditions. Without them the prerequisite will not hold. The Goal Tree is based on necessity logic as well. Nothing goes into it unless it is necessary to achieve the goal.

Existence and clarity

Third, the Logical Thinking Process requires us to <u>verify</u> the validity of the statements we make; it is not enough to have sound cause-effect relationship between entities, you must also verify their existence, or validity. Using the Current Reality Tree as an example; if we didn't find any nests in the tree, the conclusion that the tree is the reason the birds leave droppings on my windowsills would not be valid, not because the logical connection was invalid, but because there would be no birds nesting in my tree. They might of course still leave their droppings on my windows, but not because of the tree.

Fourth, the Logical Thinking Process requires us to verify possible explanations by demonstrating that not only the effect we seek to explain exists, but also that other effects that should lead from the cause proposed, actually do exist. A simple example: We think the reason an employee is reluctant to perform a specific task is that he is lazy. If this is the reason, a predicted effect is reluctance to perform other tasks as well. But if this is not the case the explanation is invalid since the predicted effect is non-existent.

Finally, clarity is really the cornerstone of every step in the Logical Thinking Process. The first question we must always ask is not only if our statements are true, but also if they are clear. What do we really mean? Does the statement reflect what we really mean? Is there any ambiguity in the statement? And if there is, we must fix that before moving on.

In H. William Dettmer's book, The *Logical Thinking Process – A Systems Approach to Complex Problem Solving,* you will find a comprehensive and detailed discussion of all the requirements that need to be fulfilled for a logical tree to be perfect. I will not go into this detail here. I will only point out, as a final remark, that in the Logical Thinking Process there are no buts and maybes. All conclusions must be based on sound logic and all explanations must be sufficiently verified. This way, we can be sure that as long as the principles are followed, our analysis will be valid by logical necessity, nothing less. And that is what makes it so damn powerful!

Finally, a word of warning: While the Logical Thinking Process may at first glance look simple and straightforward, it does in fact take rigorous training and exercise to be able to properly take advantage of it. Logic is a powerful tool, but it can also be a two-edged sword. I know that from experience.

Appendix A: A few examples

The preceding example is intended to demonstrate the whole of the Logical Thinking Process by means of a simple example. The following examples use individual parts of the process and are intended to show the variety of subjects the methodology can be applied to.

Example 1: From Symptoms to Causes

In this fictional example we work our way from a goal, through problem analysis, conflict analysis and towards a solution. The organization is a specialized hospital. The goal of our hospital is to be the leading heart surgery hospital in the region. In order to achieve this, they must hire the best people, have all necessary equipment and provide high-quality service. We see the Goal Tree below.

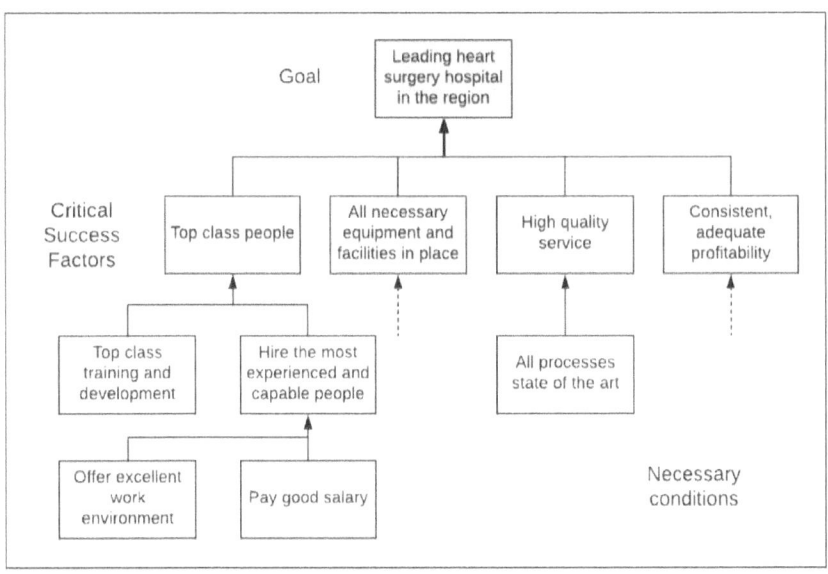

Diagram 1: Goal Tree for a hospital.

But in reality, things are not this good. The best people are leaving, financial results are getting worse and quality of the service deteriorating. In the Current Reality Tree below we see the analysis of what causes those problems. At the root of is a single KPI; salary per person. A seemingly perfectly harmless performance measure that in many systems might be fine to use. But in this system and this situation, it really drives down the performance.

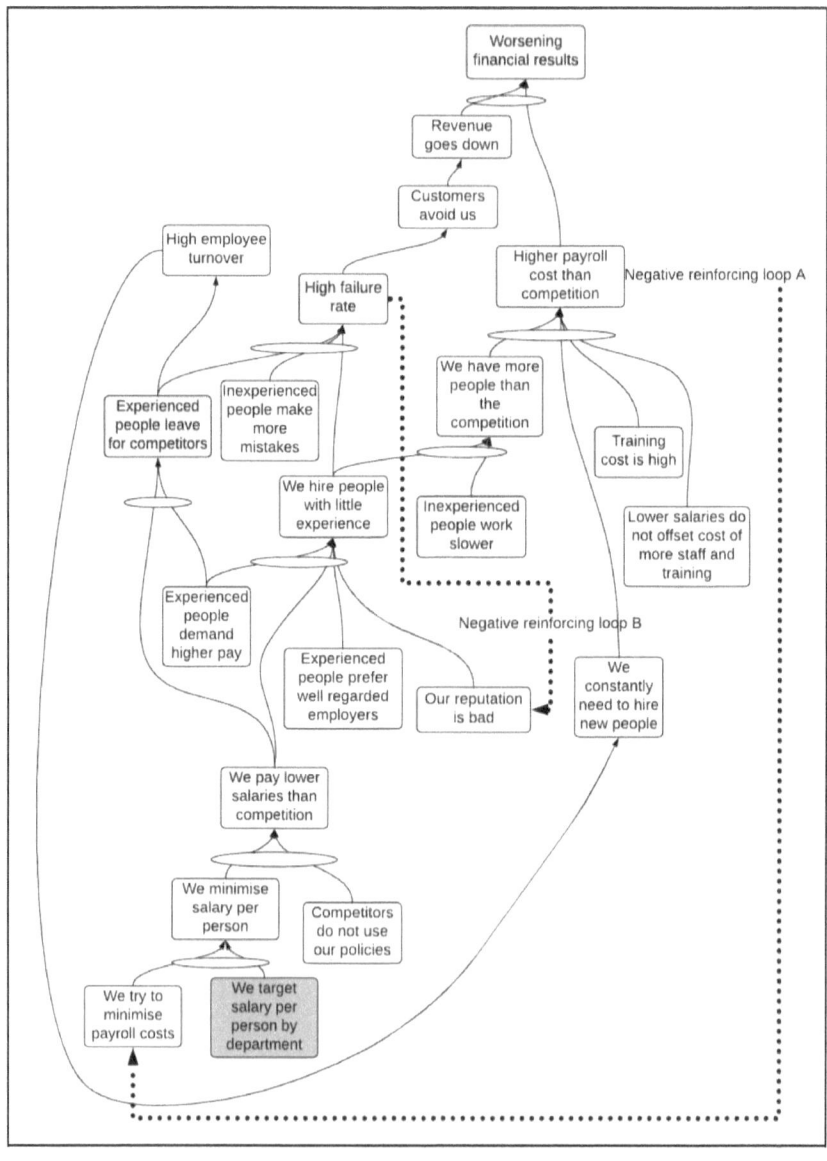

Diagram 2: Hospital Current Reality Tree.

We also see two negative reinforcing loops (vicious cycles): High payroll cost causes the need to minimize salaries (loop A), and this in turn drives high employee turnover that drives up the payroll. The high failure rate then further reinforces the reluctance of experienced people to work for the hospital, which again drives the high failure rate (loop B).

The problem with KPIs is that if used incorrectly they can cause sub-optimal performance. The reason is that many KPIs measure only results for one part of the system, ignoring the effect on the system as a whole. Salary per person measures the payroll cost only. It does not indicate the performance of the hospital at all, and even more importantly, it does not indicate the value provided by different employees. It is an overly simplistic measure and when used as an important KPI it leads to the results we have seen.

But there is an important reason we use KPIs: Running a business is to a large extent about staying in control. Keep tab on costs and revenues and being ready to take action when needed. And for a hospital payroll is a large portion of the costs. This is why we must keep it under control and hence we use the KPI of salary per person.

Now, let's imagine we are consultants working for the hospital. We show our analysis to the CEO. What is her likely reaction? Will she jump with joy and agree to throw out the problem KPI? Well, in the unlikely event she does, the CFO will surely not. He will start by asking how on earth are we then going to keep control of payroll. And chances are no-one will have an answer to that, at least not right away.

This is a classic example of a conflict; We feel we must do A, while at the same time we also feel we should avoid doing A by all means. And very often this is the end of the matter. We just live with the conflict, we keep doing things in the same old ways. In this case perhaps we just try to do some more marketing, we add some perks for employees that are cheap for us but important to them (we imagine). Perhaps we start a corporate responsibility program to try to lure people who are intrigued by such efforts. Something of the kind. But attacking the core problem? No, usually not. And why?

Perhaps it is just because we don't have the proper tools to really structure and solve the underlying conflict.

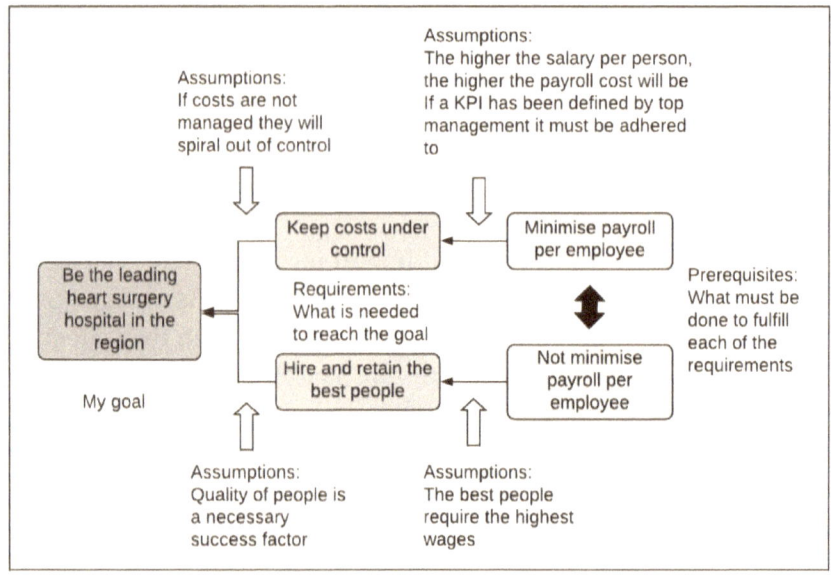

Diagram 3: The Conflict Resolution Diagram.

Now, let's structure the conflict. We start with the goal. The goal is to be the leading heart surgery hospital in the region. This is already stated. Then we formulate the opposing ends of the conflict: 1. We must base our decisions on salary per person. 2. We must not base our decisions on salary per person. Finally, we formulate the requirements by asking a simple question: Why? Why do we have to focus on salary per person? We have to in order to keep salary cost under control. And why should we not focus on it? We should not because in order to reach the goal we must hire top class people, and everyone knows top class people cost money. Driving down salary per person, more and more, will surely not attract them.

The next step is to analyze the assumptions behind the logical connections. In this case, since we have already seen the negative effects from the KPI we must focus our efforts on trying to find logical flaws in the link between the prerequisite of salary per person and the requirement of keeping costs under control. What are the assumptions here?

First, we assume we must manage costs to retain control. In essence this is true even if the methods of doing this may vary. However, this is not necessarily the only way to reach the goal. Let's say for example that we can gain a competitive advantage that allows us to charge considerably more than the competition, and/or that our processes are so good that we get a lot more utilization of resources than they do. In that case driving down costs will not be all that important. Secondly, we assume top class people are needed to run a top-class hospital. This is in fact a necessary condition we have already identified. So, the relationship between the goal and this requirement looks pretty sound. The relationship with the first requirement is more questionable.

What then about the prerequisites? We know that in general the more valuable the employee is the higher salary they will demand. Of course, there will be other factors that affect people's choice of employer, but salary is an important one and the correlation is positive. So, we already know now that we should not strive for the lowest salaries for all our people because it may go against our goal. How about the other assumptions? We assume that payroll is a big part of our costs. We assume that the higher the average salary, the higher the payroll cost will be. Finally, we assume that once a KPI has been defined it must be adhered to.

Are all those assumptions valid? Let's have a look:

Payroll is a big part of our costs. This is something we simply know. But does this necessarily mean we must manage by average salary per person? No, it does not. Even if we agree we have to keep tab on payroll the average salary is not the only way to do that. So, this assumption is not valid.

Should we manage by a KPI simply because it is required by top management? In this case, if we want to reach the goal, we should not. So, this assumption is invalid also.

What about the third one? Is salary per person the only way to keep tab on payroll? Now, salaries differ between people. We might for example decide to pay top physicians critical for our operations a higher salary than our competitors are willing to do, while keeping the salaries down for the lower-skilled employees that add less value. Overall this might still drive up payroll per person, but since we are maximizing value added, it simply does not matter.

And finally, it really is the total payroll we should focus on, not the average. The average is only part of the equation, the other part is the number of people of course. In other words, the rough average KPI we have been using is dead wrong, since it does not measure what matters for us to reach our goal. We have to find a different KPI for the payroll, if we really have to have one for it at all.

What is the morale of this story? It is simple: Our companies, institutions, societies, are systems. And to successfully manage a system we must focus on maximizing the potential of the system as a whole, not just individual parts of it. Fixing one part may or may not have an effect on the performance of the system as a whole. Even if it does, as long as we don't check against the whole we'll never know. This is why the KPIs we use must be designed in such a way that they drive the performance of the whole. If not, we will for sure end up with sub-optimal results and, often, a system ridden with conflicts.

Example 2: What is our business?

This is a recent real-life story. The company is a well established importer of hardware and tools. They had been experiencing dwindling market share and inadequate profits for quite a while. Excess stock was piling up and service to customers had deteriorated. Repeated attempts at gaining consensus on ways to improve the situation had all failed and management were in disagreement on what to do.

The first step in the analysis was to work with a group of managers and key employees to structure a Goal Tree to identify the goal and Critical Success Factors. Not surprisingly, for a for-profit business, the consensus was on the goal of improving profits, short and long term. The Critical Success Factors identified directed the team to the biggest problems, or Undesireable Effects (UDEs), the company was experiencing.

Building the Current Reality Tree took quite a bit longer than setting up the Goal Tree. The core team consisted of 3 top managers, but others were pulled in to provide the functional insights when required.

The three main tracks of analysis had to do with excess stock piling up, inadequate sales growth and slow service. All those UDEs were analyzed in detail. It soon turned out that one of the main underlying causes where the sales team was concerned was confusion and complexity due to an excess number of identical or very similar products from different vendors - sometimes they stocked as much as 10-12 such identical products. This was also a major contributing cause to overstocking. Other main causes were a lack of investment in service, only having a single sales channel to serve both resellers, contractors and individuals, and lack of effective purchasing management.

It was actually when analyzing why identical products continued to pile up, that the team identified the Critical Root Cause behind most of the problems. It turned out the reason was that when resellers started buying directly from vendors, the company usually set out to find new vendors for the products in question.

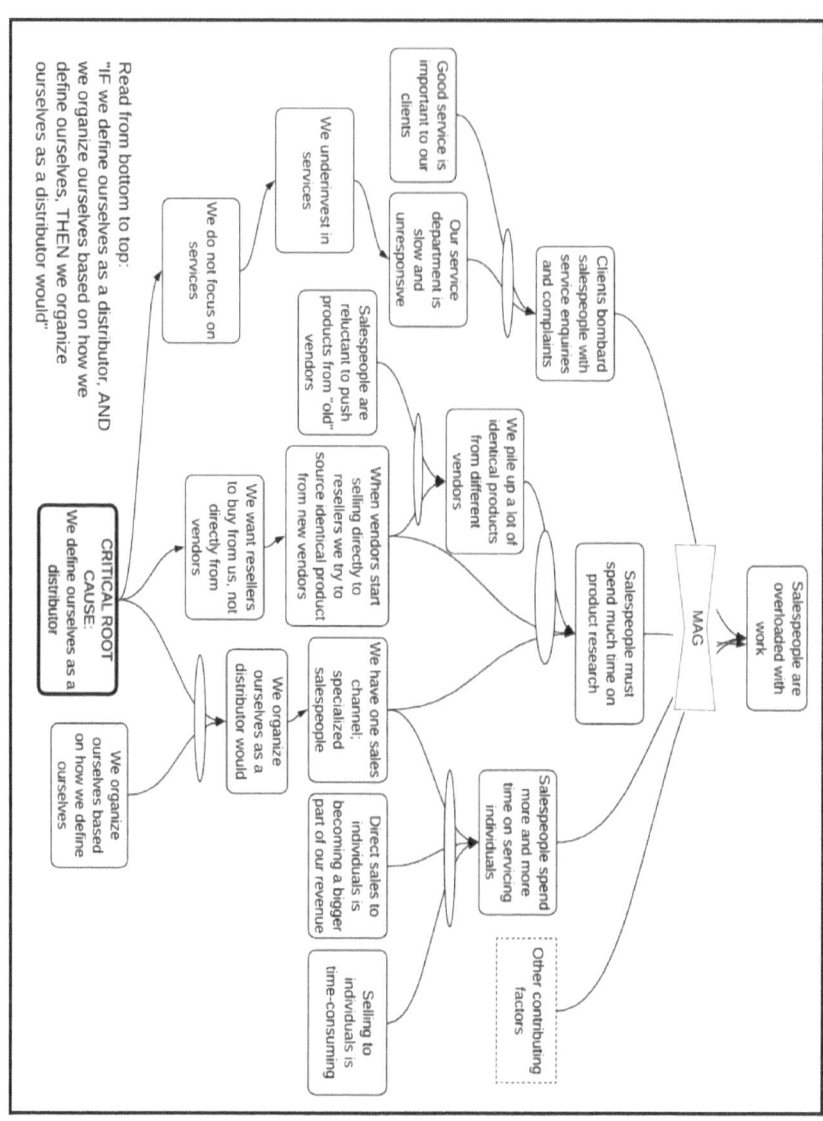

Diagram 4: „We define ourselves as a distributor". Partial, simplified Current Reality Tree. Part 1.

It was in fact an off-hand remark by the managing director, when asked about this, that led us to the solution: „Well, we define ourselves as a distributor of course. We always have been". And inherent in this view was that their retailers should buy from them, not from vendors directly. The fact, however, was that sales through resellers, once a main source of income, had become as little as a fourth of their total revenue. It also turned out that the belief that sole distributorship provided better margins was false.

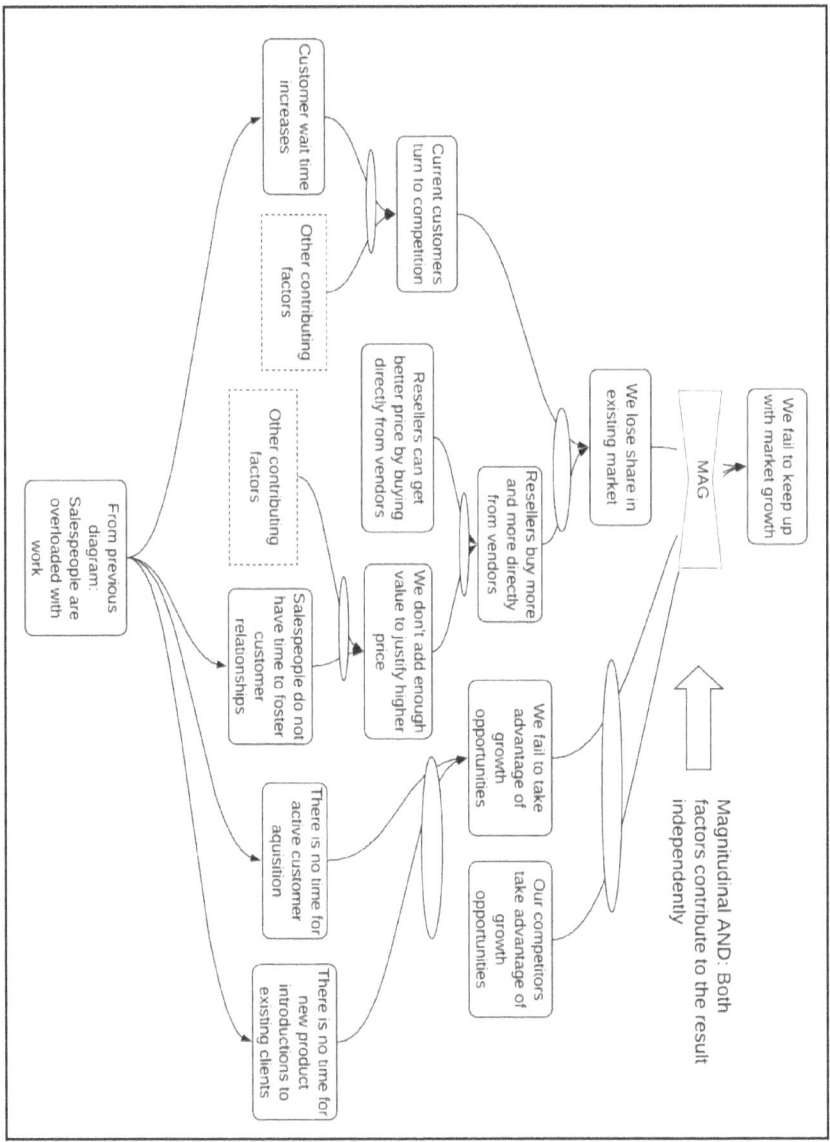

Diagram 5: „We define ourselves as a distributor". Partial, simplified Current Reality Tree. Part 2.

This Critical Root Cause, a widely shared, but false, idea of what the company's business was, was actually something nobody had expected. But as it turned out, this tacit consensus on a long-outdated definition of their business, was in fact behind most of the other problems too: Revenue was not growing because instead of using different sales channels towards different markets, they ran a single specialised sales team – as fitting for a distributor - and even if they realised they might be able to improve sales by adding more channels, they refrained from doing it so they would not upset the resellers (who actually did not matter much to them any more, and who took every opportunity to buy directly from their vendors). Service was considered as something secondary that did not really matter – this was not a key area for a distributor. We see this in the simplified Current Reality Tree below.

As often happens, once a Critical Root Cause has been identified, everything now just fell into place. And when the finished tree diagram was shared with the rest of the team the reaction was highly rewarding for those involved in constructing it: „Of course, this has been the problem the whole time. Why didn't we realise it?"

Now, the way forward was clear. Plans were made to add new sales channels, restructure the purchasing process, invest in better service capabilities and set up a business development function to seek out new opportunities. And this time, the plans were actually put in motion: A year after the first steps in the Logical Thinking Process analysis were taken, the company is now on a fast track forward with a clear goal and strong consensus on what needs to be done to achieve it.

How likely is it that this situation would have been solved without the Logical Thinking Process analysis? Would any amount of financial analysis have led to this conclusion and the common understanding of its significance? Of course it would not have. The difference between the Logical Thinking Process and the methods most often used is that as a qualitative, not quantitative, analysis framework, the LTP really helps unearth not just faulty financial ratios or broken processes. It helps getting to the false beliefs and paradigms that so often are the real cause of the problems experienced.

Example 3: Why is systemic thinking so important

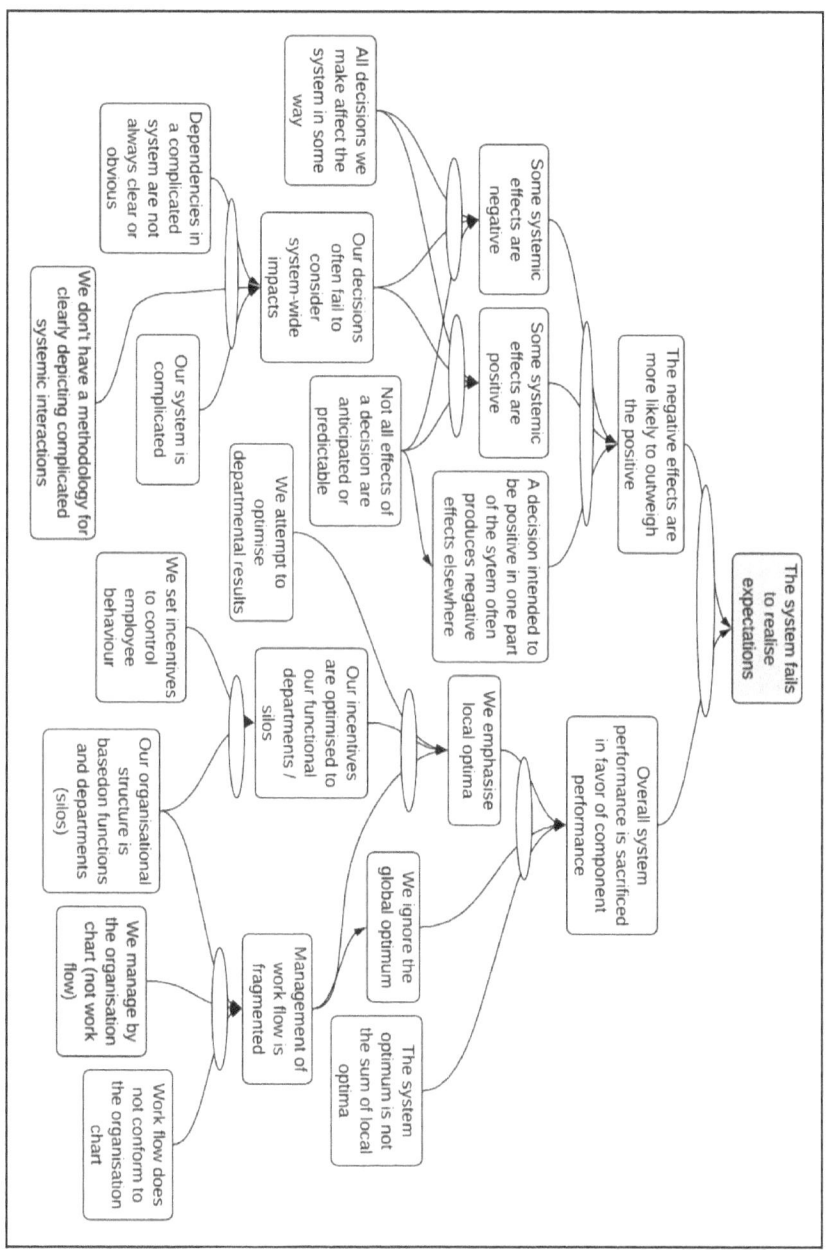

Diagram 7: What drives sub-optimal system results?

Every organization is a complicated system. In such a system, what happens somewhere in the system affects the situation elsewhere, but it can be overwhelmingly difficult to figure out what those effects will be. Our organizations are usually organized functionally, and they are hierarchical in nature.

But the functional division and hierarchies do not reflect the workings of the system, often they rather cloud the true causality within it. The Current Reality Tree depicted here explains how sub-optimal results are caused by two critical root causes: The tendency to manage by the organizational chart and the lack of proper tools to analyze cause-effect relationships within the system.[6] One of those root causes can be addressed by the Logical Thinking Process. And chances are, once that is done, the other one will be addressed too.

Appendix B: The flow and logic of the process

When applying the Logical Thinking Process, it is crucial to adhere to the logical principles that apply to each step in the process. The diagram on the following page is intended as a comprehensive guide to the process. It explains the purpose of each step, the questions asked, the type of logic used, and a checklist intended to aid the user when building the analysis. The checklist is even more important when it comes to scrutinizing and validating the analysis. Each entity and each logical connection must be validated based on the checklist. It takes a good amount of training to be able to quickly build a valid logical analysis, especially when it is complicated. The checklist is useful for this purpose.

	1. Goal Tree	2. Current Reality Tree
Purpose	Define a goal, critical success factors and necessary conditions for achieving it.	Define the symptoms and determine critical root causes behind them. A root cause will often consist in a faulty assumption or in a conflict.
Questions asked and actions taken	What is the goal? What is truly necessary to achieve it (no nice-to-haves)? If some of the critical success factors or necessary conditions are not in place, go to step 2 to analyse why.	What are the root level causes behind the symptoms identified and are they sufficient to produce them? How, precisely, do the root causes lead to the symptoms? If there is a conflict, go to step 3. If not, go directly to step 3.
Type of reasoning	Necessity logic (In order to ... We must)	Sufficiency logic (If ... Then)
Validity checklist (categories of legitimate reservations): Follow this list to check the validity for each entity and each connection in the logic trees.	Is any additional explanation required for the cause, or effect, as written?	Is any additional explanation required for the cause, or effect, as written?
	Is the connection between cause and effect convincing at face value?	Is the connection between cause and effect convincing at face value?
	Are any intermediate effects missing between cause and effect?	Are any intermediate effects missing between cause and effect?
	Is the statement in each entity a complete idea?	Is the statement in each entity a complete idea?
	Is the statement structurally sound; that is, does it express only one idea in a single entity, is there no embedded if-then statement within the entity?	Is the statement structurally sound; that is, does it express only one idea in a single entity, is there no embedded if-then statement within the entity?
	Does the statement seem valid?	Does the statement seem valid?
	Does the cause really result in the effect when read out as an if-then statement?	Does the cause really result in the effect when read out as an if-then statement?
		If the cause is intangible, can an additional predicted effect be identified?
	Is the cause sufficient to produce the effect or are other causes needed too?	Is the cause sufficient to produce the effect or are other causes needed too?
	Is the cause really necessary to produce the effect; is it certain that the effect will not be produced if the cause does not exist?	
	Is the cause the only possible cause or could something else produce the effect by itself?	Is the cause the only possible cause or could something else produce the effect by itself?
	Is the cause really causing the effect, or is the stated effect in fact causing the stated cause?	Is the cause really causing the effect, or is the stated effect in fact causing the stated cause?
		What other effects should lead from the cause, and do they exist?
	Is there circular logic in the cause-effect relationship?	Is there circular logic in the cause-effect relationship?

3. Conflict Resolution Diagram	4. Future Reality Tree	5. Prerequisite Tree
Structure, then analyse conflicts that may lie behind critical root causes and come up with injections to solve them	Analyse if injections to conflicts and/or direct solutions to critical root causes are sufficient to achieve the goal	Define precisely, when needed, all the steps necessary to realise each entity in step 4
What are the conflicts behind critical root causes? Do the conflicts really exist? What are the logical connections between the entities in the CRD and are all those connections valid? What may be done differently to eliminate the conflicts? Use those suggestions as inputs in step 4.	Are the injections or direct solutions really sufficient to achieve the goal or is something more needed? How precisely will they lead to this? Are there any negative effects resulting from the solutions? If some entities need further step-by-step analysis, go to step 5.	What are the necessary steps to realise each entity? Are there obstacles on the way? How can those obstacles be removed? When done, use the Prerequisite Tree as a basis for a project plan.
Necessity logic (In order to ... We must)	Sufficiency logic (If ... Then)	Necessity logic (In order to ... We must)
Is any additional explanation required for the cause, or effect, as written?	Is any additional explanation required for the cause, or effect, as written?	Is any additional explanation required for the cause, or effect, as written?
Is the connection between cause and effect convincing at face value?	Is the connection between cause and effect convincing at face value?	Is the connection between cause and effect convincing at face value?
Are any intermediate effects missing between cause and effect?	Are any intermediate effects missing between cause and effect?	Are any intermediate effects missing between cause and effect?
Is the statement in each entity a complete idea?	Is the statement in each entity a complete idea?	Is the statement in each entity a complete idea?
Is the statement structurally sound; that is, does it express only one idea in a single entity, is there no embedded if-then statement within the entity?	Is the statement structurally sound; that is, does it express only one idea in a single entity, is there no embedded if-then statement within the entity?	Is the statement structurally sound; that is, does it express only one idea in a single entity, is there no embedded if-then statement within the entity?
Does the statement seem valid?	Does the statement seem valid?	Does the statement seem valid?
Does the cause really result in the effect when read out as an if-then statement?	Does the cause really result in the effect when read out as an if-then statement?	Does the cause really result in the effect when read out as an if-then statement?
If the cause is intangible, can an additional predicted effect be identified?		
Is the cause sufficient to produce the effect or are other causes needed too?	Is the cause sufficient to produce the effect or are other causes needed too?	Is the cause sufficient to produce the effect or are other causes needed too?
Is the cause really necessary to produce the effect; is it certain that the effect will not be produced if the cause does not exist?		Is the cause really necessary to produce the effect; is it certain that the effect will not be produced if the cause does not exist?
Is the cause the only possible cause or could something else produce the effect by itself?		
Is the cause really causing the effect, or is the stated effect in fact causing the stated cause?	Is the cause really causing the effect, or is the stated effect in fact causing the stated cause?	
What other effects should lead from the cause, and do they exist?	What other effects should lead from the cause, and do they exist?	
Is there circular logic in the cause-effect relationship?	Is there circular logic in the cause-effect relationship?	Is there circular logic in the cause-effect relationship?

Epilogue: A few points on language

How language is both the basis of critical thinking and its worst enemy

"Language is the root of all misunderstandings."
(Antoine de Saint-Exupéry)

"We have minds that are equipped for certainty, linearity and short-term decisions, that must instead make long-term decisions in a non-linear, probabilistic world."
(Paul Gibbons)

Language is the tool we use for communication. But words and sentences can have vague and ambiguous meaning and different individuals most often understand what is expressed in different ways. Therefore, lack of clarity and precision often leads to misunderstandings that again lead to conflicts, and imprecise use of language can often limit our ability to express our thoughts accurately. Using a framework based on sound deductive logic can greatly help to clarify our communication.

In the workplace and in private life we often experience problems that, in the end are not actually problems, but only symptoms of underlying issues. However, we all have a very strong tendency to jump straight from a superficial and inadequate analysis into actions that only aim at tackling consequences instead of causes. The result is that the improvement we seek often comes to nothing.

It also often happens that the problems we face have a few common roots, which we fail to notice. They can even all have the same cause, but because we are unable to properly analyze the causality we fail to find real and lasting solutions. And often the root lies in a conflict that we can actually solve, as long as we are able to identify it.

The Logical Thinking Process is a framework we can use to clarify our thoughts and make our communication more effective. This may be in the corporate environment where ambiguity often stalls progress. It has also been used with children in the classroom to solve conflicts and help them better realize their own goals and how to achieve them.

Just think of the advantage we would give our children if we trained them to logically formulate their thoughts and think through their decisions to the end.

And what about the ambiguities, complexity and misinformation we experience in the adult world? The prejudice and hatred, the sloppy decision making that leads us into misfortune? The conflicts we run into just because we don't think clearly?

We all have the ability to think logically. The Logical Thinking Process provides us with the tools to do this in a structured way and thus helps us better deal with the complex world we live in.

And we are all able to ask the questions that underpin the Logical Thinking Process:

> *"Why do I have this?"*

> *"Why should I do this?"*

And last but not least:

> **"What do you really mean?"**

So why not start there?

Reading on

The most comprehensive source for those interested in learning more is without doubt *"The Logical Thinking Process - A Systems Approach to Complex Problem Solving"* by H. William Dettmer.

Other good books on the subject include Dettmer's shorter version, *"The Logical Thinking Process - An Executive Summary"*, *"Thinking for a Change"*, by Lisa Scheinkopf, *"Management Dilemmas"* by Eli Schragenheim, and of course Eli Goldratt's "The Goal" which, among other things, introduces the way of structuring our thinking that the Logical Thinking Process is based on.

I would also recommend the Goal Systems website, http://logicalthinkingprocess.com which has a lot of interesting material, the Marris Consulting website, https://www.marris-consulting.com/en/our-videos-about-logical-thinking-process and Christian Hohmann's blog https://hohmannchris.wordpress.com

Acknowledgments

Many thanks to H. William (Bill) Dettmer and Christian Hohmann for all their valuable inputs and constructive criticism during the process of pulling together the contents of this book, and to Bill for taking the time to thoroughly review the finished manuscript. Many thanks to John Stretch, consultant and FP&A expert, for his review and valuable feedback. Special thanks to professor Jón Torfi Jónasson, University of Iceland, for his invaluable advice. And last but not least, many thanks to my wife Margret for carefully reviewing the final proof and suggesting important improvements.

About the author

I am an Icelandic entrepreneur, writer and educator with a strong track-record in software, strategy consulting and performance management. I am an INSEAD MBA and a philosophy major as well as being a certified expert in the Logical Thinking Process.

I live in Reykjavik, Iceland, and divide my time between managing a software business, providing consulting and training, writing and research.

If you are interested in finding out where to look in your area for proper training or qualified assistance in the Logical Thinking Process, or just want to have a chat, please don't hesitate to get in touch.

Contact me at thorsteinn.siglaugsson@insead.edu, call +354-659-9910 or get in touch through LinkedIn. I will only be happy to help.

[1] https://www.mckinsey.com/business-functions/organization/our-insights/how-to-beat-the-transformation-odds

[2] https://www.imdb.com/title/tt5471480/

[3] It is important also to consider the relationship between the goal, the purpose, or nature of the system as such, and the critical success factors and necessary condition. The goal may or may not include the purpose or nature of the system, but the critical success factors and the necessary conditions will always be affected by the nature of the system. Let's clarify this: Imagine our system is a bookstore. Then let's say we define the goal as simply making more money now and in the future. No reference to the bookstore here. But the conditions necessary to fulfill this goal will always be affected by what the system is. One might be to offer a wide enough selection of books to fulfill the needs of our target market. Another might have to do with keeping control of inventory. And so on; all will be related to what it is we do, even if the goal is a very generic one. On the other hand, we might decide to include the system description, mission or purpose in the goal statement as such. Offering the widest selection of science fiction books in town might be an example of such a goal. The money part might then be a critical success factor or even a necessary condition (for the goal will of course not be reached if the bookstore goes bust).

[4] Now someone might say: "Ok, this is perhaps the logical thing to do, but all the same, I just might want to keep the tree despite all the problems." Such a response does in no way invalidate the logical analysis carried out, but it indicates yet another assumption, in this case an emotional attachment to precisely this tree. Perhaps it was planted by your grandmother, it might remind you of your children climbing in it when they were little... If this is the case the new assumption should be added and probably a new injection would have to be found.

[5] A valid necessity statement might look like this: „In order for my windows to remain dirty something must soil them and I must not clean them."

[6] Current Reality Tree developed in co-operation with H. William Dettmer